Quebec in a
New World

Quebec in a New World

The National Executive Council of the Parti Québécois

Translated by Robert Chodos

James Lorimer & Company, Publishers
Toronto, 1994

Originally published as *Le Québec dans un Monde Nouveau*
©1993 VLB Éditeur
Translation ©1994 by Robert Chodos

James Lorimer & Company Ltd. acknowledges with thanks the support of the Canada Council, the Ontario Arts Council and the Ontario Publishing Centre in the development of writing and publishing in Canada.

Canadian Cataloguing in Publication Data

Parti quebecois
   Quebec in a New World

Translation of: Le Quebec dans un monde nouveau.
ISBN 1-55028-445-2 (bound) ISBN 1-55028-444-4 (pbk.)

1. Quebec (Province) - History - Autonomy and independence movements. 2. Sovereignty - Economic aspects - Quebec (Province). 3. Quebec (Province) - Politics and government - 1985-   .*
4. Federal-provincial relations - Quebec (Province).*
I. Title.

FC2925.9.S37P3813 1994   971.4'04 C94-930918-4
F1053.2.S37P3813 1994

James Lorimer & Company Ltd., Publishers
35 Britain Street
Toronto, Ontario M5A 1R7

Printed and bound in Canada

Contents

Foreword

This volume makes available for the first time in English the detailed plan of how the Parti Québécois sees Quebec achieving independence in 1995. Readers will discover that the PQ no longer makes negotiating an economic association with Ottawa a condition of attaining independence. It is now saying it will take Quebec's future in its own hands. In office, a PQ government will, first, ask the Quebec National Assembly to pass a resolution affirming the goal of independence; and, second, create a constitutional commission to define powers for the newly independent state. In a subsequent referendum, the Quebec population will be asked to approve sovereignty and the constitutional framework for independence.

Opting for Independence

The PQ document presented here is divided into three parts. In Part I, the party outlines its principal concerns. It argues that the emerging global economy is forcing rapid change on all societies. But Canadian federalism is a significant barrier to Quebec making the changes it needs in order to find its place in the new world order. For example, the creation of a new economic space in North America gives Quebec an incentive to rethink policies on training and education, and economic infrastructure.

International trade creates economies of scale but costs jobs. A coherent response requires national policies to create jobs; Canada cannot act because the fundamental disagreements that mar federalism block the major adjustments needed.

The PQ argues that meeting the challenge of new global trends requires the instruments of sovereignty. Part II sets out national goals for Quebec. Rather than give up state power in a new international environment characterized by the creation of large economic blocs, the PQ argues that it is most important to redefine government power. Many of the traditional tools of national economic development have already been rendered inoperative by the GATT, FTA, and NAFTA; but a neoconservative outlook, allowing international market forces full sway over the economy and society, makes little sense. Instead, a new set of interventionist policies is needed. A small unitary state could better deliver the needed response than a large federal state hamstrung by existing conflicts.

For the PQ, the new Quebec must be built on partnerships and social solidarities. It will feature equality of opportunity and pluralism as important values. The common will to live together is what distinguishes Quebec. It can be promoted by a new commitment to people and to local communities and cities in all regions. Part III explains how Quebec's accession to sovereignty will take place. It defines

Quebec citizenship and addresses the issues that will arise during the transition to independence, including the division of the property and debt, and the maintenance of economic union.

Playing for New Stakes

In the 1980s, the Canadian constitutional debate was about renewing federalism. In Quebec, the option of renewed federalism was designed to counter the PQ's option of sovereignty. With the failure of the Meech Lake Accord, and the temporary withdrawal of the Quebec government from constitutional negotiations, the modalities of independence were clarified by the work of the all-party Bélanger-Campeau commission. Bill 150 of the Quebec National Assembly set out a procedure for a public consultation on sovereignty, although it was the Charlottetown Accord that was eventually put to the people in a separate Quebec referendum. The defeat of the accord was interpreted by Quebec sovereignists as closing the door on renewed federalism as an alternative to independence.

Today, the constitutional debate has once again returned to the issue of sovereignty. Non-partisan preparatory work for the constitutional debate clarified how Quebec could achieve independence. The concept and meaning of sovereignty was the subject of expert study and discussion within the context of elaborating the Quebec government's position for constitutional reform. The debate surrounding sovereignty was enlarged beyond the confines of the PQ. It became an option for a wider segment of society, including elements of the business class, than ever before.

Following the defeat of the Charlottetown agreement, amending the Canadian constitution is no longer on the national political agenda. By default, the options facing Canada have narrowed to federalism versus Quebec independence. In parliament, Quebec independence is championed by the leader of the official opposition. Yet, apart from Lucien Bouchard, outside Quebec, the existing federal state is taken for granted in political debate. Constitutional fatigue is commonly cited as the reason why much of what has happened within Quebec has gone without comment in other parts of the country.

In a sense, the debate over Quebec's future has come back to the heady days following the Quiet Revolution. The year 1968 saw the creation of the Parti Québécois. At that time, the option of outright independence was very much alive in Quebec nationalist circles. But dissident Quebec Liberal supporters of René Lévesque, and those committed to Quebec separation, agreed to unite behind the idea of sovereignty-association. Though a strong nationalist impulse was the basis for the PQ program, those opposed to an economic association with Canada were silenced. The openly separatist element was marginalized. In preparing for its electoral victory in 1976, the PQ put forward a policy of first promising good government; and only after holding a referendum asking the Quebec population to give the PQ a mandate to negotiate sovereignty-association.

With its defeat in the 1980 referendum, the PQ embarked temporarily on a new course: reconciliation of its nationalist project with constitutional reform. It identified itself as promoting the traditional Quebec negotiating objective: more powers for Quebec within Canada; and took a role with other provinces in opposing the consitutional proposals of the Trudeau Liberals. The political fallout from the 1982 repatriation package, eventually accepted by all provincial governments except Quebec, was significant for the PQ. Lévesque departed the leadership in June 1985, and his successor, the moderate Pierre-Marc Johnson, lost the election in December 1985 to the Quebec Liberals, led once again by Robert Bourassa.

The principal opponents of the PQ in the 1982 battle over the constitution, the federal Liberals, lost their electoral base in Quebec to the Mulroney Tories in 1984. Quebec nationalist support was a major factor in the two Mulroney victories. With Trudeau retired, Mulroney and Bourassa worked together to promote renewed federalism, but with no visible success. When Pierre-Marc Johnson was replaced as leader of the PQ by Jacques Parizeau, the party went back to its sovereignty agenda.

The New Agenda

Throughout its history, one question has been insistently posed whenever the PQ has raised sovereignty. That question is: What are the economic consequences? The arguments that are taken up in the following document do not always focus on what we may expect. Rather than emphasizing how Canada has failed to accommodate its French-Canadian citizens, for example, the arguments focus on the options for economic renewal. In 1994, it is the PQ that is posing the question: What is the economic future of Quebec within a divided Canada?

The PQ accepts in a matter-of-fact way the new alignment of economic forces in North America and the world. Its leaders assume that the creation of a North American economic space holds out new prospects for those that know how to take advantage of them. They fear that in a world of economic blocs, while other countries will make the necessary modifications to their policies, Canada and its provinces will not. In these circumstances the PQ argues that Quebec is better to go ahead with its own national project.

A sovereign Quebec would gather all its own tax revenues, make all its own laws, join international organizations, and negotiate international treaties. An independent Quebec would disengage from Canadian federalism while taking on most of the responsibilities currently exercised by Ottawa. Quebec would continue to use the Canadian dollar as its currency and maintain the existing tariffs against the rest of the world. Quebec would also want to preserve the freedom of movement of goods, services, capital and people (what it calls "the economic space") it shares with the other Canadian provinces. Matters that would require ongoing regulation and discussion — for instance, transport and communication — could be dealt with by joint commissions established between Quebec and Canada.

This document argues that formal association with Canada would be desirable for the exercise of Quebec's sovereignty. But it also suggests that the economic interests of Canada would make cooperation inevitable.

The obvious political response to the PQ is to create jobs, improve the economic outlook and show that federalism works. This, indeed, is what Prime Minister Chrétien has said he intends to do. But the issue is more than simply showing that Canadians have the political skills needed to live together and that governments have an economic strategy for hard times. The issue raised by the PQ is, What kind of society can best meet the challenges of a world in which little is guaranteed? Their answer is first that a viable society requires a state that can affirm its distinctiveness and strengthen it economically and, second, that for Quebec the constitutional status quo is a threat to both these goals. Quebec society wants to join the world and the PQ sees Canada's political system as an obsolete and crippling barrier to Quebec's self-definition.

The 1995 Referendum

The issue of Quebec independence will undoubtedly be closely judged by Quebecers. The PQ must first win the confidence of the population as a government, and then win it again when it puts its constitutional proposals to a vote. The federal Liberals can hardly remain indifferent to the challenge posed by the PQ program. The Bloc Québécois is intent on countering any participation by Jean Chrétien and his Liberals in the referendum debate. Its fifty-four members of the federal parliament add an important political contingent in support of the PQ.

Reaction outside Quebec to what is being proposed here will not be without significance. The initial response is likely to cover the spectrum from astonishment to frustration, to indifference and disbelief, but some will want to engage in a dialogue with the PQ. The desire to debate the PQ on specific points is probably the natural response from other provincial governments and federalist parties outside Quebec. And there is much material here for debate. This book, prepared by the PQ for the Quebec public, tells readers clearly what independence will entail.

In the coming debate over Quebec sovereignty it is important to understand as fully as possible what exactly is being proposed. But for myself, as editor of *The Canadian Forum,* and for others who have taken part in encouraging Canada's debates for over twenty years, the issues raised here by the PQ have a resonance that goes beyond the form of the Canadian state or the meaning of federalism. Anyone concerned about Canadian sovereignty in a global economy can benefit from considering the issues raised in this book. Open democratic debate is an end in itself and the PQ has made an important contribution with this publication.

Quebec in a New World helps identify those questions that will define our future. Most important, its publication signals a desire to maintain a civilized dialogue on a subject that generates great emotions and not a little misunderstanding. People of good will, whatever their ultimate conclusions about the merits of the positions exposed here, can only welcome the opportunity afforded to deepen their understanding of the aspirations of Quebec sovereignists.

Duncan Cameron

Preface

Quebec society is going through a difficult period. Its ways of life and habits of mind are being challenged from all sides. Thirty years of progress and achievements are now being questioned. The achievements have become a source of problems; the progress appears to be disintegrating.

Thirty years ago, educational reform was the starting point of the Quiet Revolution. But now we are facing the weaknesses of our education system: a growing school dropout rate, functional illiteracy and the collapse of vocational training at the secondary level. After investing so much energy and money to ensure that education would be accessible to all our young people, how can we explain such disappointing results?

In the last thirty years, a group of ambitious and innovative entrepreneurs has appeared in Quebec. Supported by a strong network of public, cooperative and private institutions, this rising class seemed to have the future in its grasp; people believed that its initiatives would overcome all obstacles. Now, a number of the big names among the new entrepreneurs have gone under, and there is a growing impression that the rising class as a whole is faltering.

Regional development policies gave rise to the hope that Quebec's regions would become less dependent on natural resources, which were often too quickly depleted, and better able to stem the rural exodus that had drained them. The regions would be resurrected, it seemed, but it was not long before disenchantment set in. Young people continued to leave, and unease became increasingly widespread.

People also began to sense that the poor were becoming both poorer and more numerous, and the facts eventually confirmed their suspicions. They began to speak of a Quebec divided in two. The unemployment rate rose, and bringing it down seemed impossible.

In general, Quebec's great social achievements have been called into question. Can we still afford the welfare state? Even more broadly, will today's generation of young people be the first who will not live as well as their parents? Is it not then irresponsible to make this generation bear the real burden of today's deficits? The background for these questions is a neoconservative ideology claiming to be an expression of protest against a ubiquitous and bloated government that regulates everything. In this context, there is a tendency to throw out the baby with the bathwater and allow market forces to dissolve social responsibility and break social solidarity.

People point out that other societies are also undergoing the same developments and experiencing the same realizations, conclusions, worries and reappraisals. This is no doubt true, although to different degrees in different places. However, a significant number of these societies retain a capacity for change, movement and hope.

This is not so in Canada. Government, which in the past played a central role in the cultural, social and political spheres, now finds itself at a standstill. There has been much critical comment about the way rivalry between the two major levels of government, federal and provincial, leads to duplication and waste. In the end, the result is a kind of sclerosis that makes any effort painful and limited if not impossible. Paralysis is no way to live.

That is our situation. For five years, all of Canada's governments engaged in an effort to change the system, create new hope and rediscover a zest for leadership, but the failure of the Charlottetown Accord marked the end of that initiative. No longer will anyone seek hope or try to find a way forward through renewed Canadian federalism.

It is in this context that the executive council of the Parti Québécois is issuing this position paper. It has three sections. The first explores the challenges that societies such as Quebec today cannot escape. The second presents what can be called, for want of a less presumptuous term, a *projet de société* — a plan for the kind of society we would like to create. This section makes clear that only in a sovereign Quebec will it be possible to implement this plan. The third section seeks to explore one of the major discoveries of our time: that a small society can prosper and develop as long as it forms part of a large market. Economic association with the rest of Canada, in the context of an expanding North American economic space, can be defined and articulated without compromising the goal of sovereignty.

This position paper will serve its purpose if it inspires people to think about the future and re-awakens,in those who have become disheartened or cynical a taste for change and constructive action.

Jacques Parizeau

The Challenges of a New World

Quebec is part of a new world. Everywhere around us, countries and continents are changing. Economic strategies, social relations and cultural trends transcend national borders and take shape on a planetary scale. A new order is rapidly emerging and making its presence felt everywhere on earth.

The new environment affects both the internal organization of societies and the relationships among them. Societies everywhere need to adjust, and this adjustment involves both our institutions and the values on which our traditions and cultures are based. In the last few years, vast transformations have shaken and even brought down what had appeared to be unchangeable institutions, created new global economic alliances, reunited what had previously been divided nations and freed others of political superstructures that had become obsolete.

These transformations have substantially modified the nature and meaning of borders throughout the world. In economic terms, a country's domestic market is no longer enough to ensure prosperity for its population or viability for many of its industries. As a result, nation-states have increasingly resorted to international treaties guaranteeing access to one another's domestic markets. They have also established a new network of international economic institutions responsible for overseeing, and sometimes for administering, the bilateral, continental and international trade agreements around which the new world economic order is being built.

Governments and the New World Economic Order

The rapid development of large economic blocs has forced governments to respect the new rules of the game. Some of the instruments governments have traditionally relied on to stimulate economic development are now closed to them, while others can be used only with difficulty. Whereas governments used to be able to encourage local industries by guaranteeing them a share of the domestic market through import quotas or high tariff walls, trade agreements now all but prohibit the use of instruments of this sort. It is also becoming clear that in the near future direct and even indirect subsidies to business will be forbidden or at least severely circumscribed by the rules of international trade.

Some people have argued that these international trends sound the death knell for the role of government in the economy and indirectly in other areas of social organization as well. This neoconservative ideology was put into practice in some places, but its limitations soon became apparent. Quebec adheres to the principles of a market economy, but we do not consider it an option for the Quebec government simply to stand and watch the trends taking shape at a world level, without lending its weight to ensure respect for the trade rules that are in force. The government can, and must, act to help achieve the conditions of economic success.

A society such as Quebec can hope to win the gamble of globalized markets only if it can formulate — and, even more important, implement — coherent adjustment strategies. In this sense, it is not the new international environment that represents a threat to our society as much as the refusal to adjust to it and bring about the changes that are needed.

An effort to adjust to globalization implies changes that will affect every dimension of present-day Quebec. It is not only our methods of production that will need reexamination. We will also have to take a new look at the systems and institutions through which we work out common projects and mobilize our resources to implement them. In other words, putting into effect a conventional economic development strategy will not be enough. Rather, our effort needs to take the form of a genuine *projet de société*, a social plan based on a broad consensus and serving as a backdrop to everything the government and its partners do.

In its economic dimension, this plan will of course be primarily concerned with companies and their employees, who will be on the front lines of competition in domestic and foreign markets. But we have no intention of sending them to the front alone. Government action needs to focus on a few essential areas. The first is a massive effort to upgrade our human resources and retrain our workers. In light of accelerating technological change, this effort should be directed towards offering adequate vocational training both to people who currently have jobs and to those who need to be reintegrated into the labour market.

The government will also need to invest in infrastructure, especially transportation infrastructure and public works, to create a physical environment favourable to economic development. To promote the availability of capital, it will need to make sure that a variety of solid financial institutions are present in each region. Another important area of action will be offering tangible support to companies in their efforts to penetrate export markets. Our exports should be more diversified, and we should be exporting more high-value-added products. To achieve this, we need to encourage research and innovation in all economic sectors, which means that the curiosity, creativity and initiative of Quebecers, and especially young Quebecers, should be a high priority.

Political Structures that Meet
the Challenge of Globalization

Strategies that consist of increasing, or even simply maintaining, current levels of protection of domestic markets will never represent a viable response in the present international context. What is needed to prevent the transition to a global economy from leading to the economic and social breakdown of

entire regions is a strategy that is actively supported by government and can mobilize all the people concerned.] This is the context in which the
question of the political future of Quebec needs to be
raised. The challenge confronting us is a formidable
one. Meeting it will require all the forces in our
society to mobilize and act together in a way they
never have before.

The signing of the Canada-U.S. Free Trade Agreement (FTA) was neither the first nor the last step in
the creation of a North American economic bloc.
Even before the FTA was signed, a significant portion of Canada-U.S. trade was carried out free of
tariffs, notably under the Autopact and the most-favoured-nation provision of the General Agreement
on Tariffs and Trade (GATT). The integration of
Mexico into the North American free trade zone
through the North American Free Trade Agreement
(NAFTA) will accelerate the process, and trade lib-
eralization under the Uruguay Round of GATT, concluded in late 1993, will be another factor to contend
with. As a result of these events, Quebec will need to
develop clearer strategies and define the *projet de
société* on which these strategies will be based. The
same is true for English Canada, which faces the
same economic issues in its own way and its own
particular context.

Under the current political structures that Quebec and English Canada share for better or for
worse, it is becoming increasingly clear that strategies of this sort cannot be put into effect without
endless jurisdictional quarrels, conflicts over priorities and sterile constitutional debates. Instead of

mobilizing us to pursue common projects, our institutions divide us and prevent us from taking action. Instead of ensuring that our economy and our public affairs are managed efficiently, they encourage an appalling level of duplication and overlap that soaks up precious resources of time and money.

Artificially maintaining a structure that all evidence suggests is obsolete and powerless to implement an adjustment strategy is not in English Canada's interest any more than it is in Quebec's. A number of essential components of any such strategy are constitutionally under provincial jurisdiction. English Canada might like to use a strengthened federal government, with sufficient resources at its disposal to fulfil its ambitions, as an instrument to put national strategies in sectors such as education, occupational training and telecommunications into effect. However, such an approach would be unacceptable to Quebec. For us, any such strategies would have to be carried out by the Quebec government, which in the current political framework also lacks the resources to fulfil its legitimate ambitions.

Thus, the Canadian federal system is a major obstacle to the pursuit of the goals of both societies. Quebec and English Canada are caught in a constitutional trap that prevents both of them from enjoying the benefits of their sovereignty and adopting strategies to meet the most important challenges of our time. Canada is at an impasse, and it is clearly in the interest of both partners to get out of this impasse as quickly as possible.

The Differing Roles of Big and Small Business in Economic Development

Job creation has to be the top priority of any government intervention in the economy. The increasing openness of economies and the globalization of trade are not the only major shifts that affect us. The dynamics of job creation have also changed considerably, calling into question the very nature of economic policy.

For a long time, industrialized countries depended heavily on sectoral policies primarily aimed at taking advantage of cost reduction achieved through economies of scale. As a result, these countries ended up with a steadily growing number of large automated production units. Large corporations rapidly increased their share of international trade, but at the same time, their share of employment declined.

In this context, small business quickly became the major source of new jobs in most industrialized countries. Investment by large transnational corporations took the form of a sudden massive infusion of capital, which created a substantial number of jobs during the construction phase. But over the medium and long term, the direct effect of the resulting production units on employment was relatively modest. Large corporations often had the most significant impact on employment through subcontracting to local small business in the regions where they carried out production. In addition, international competition forced these corporations to modernize their machinery on a regular basis, and this usually meant a net reduction in jobs.

Large corporations have still been the engines of economic development. It is often because of them that small businesses proliferate, and they make it possible to penetrate major trade markets. Especially when access to international markets is an essential condition of a prosperous economy, it is extremely important for a people to own and control a substantial number of the large corporations that shape its economy.

While a new factory or subsidiary established by a large foreign corporation represents a significant asset for a country, it is considerably more advantageous to be home to the corporation's head office and all the activities that go along with it. A country is then not limited to executing simple tasks. It can benefit from activities and jobs that are major generators of value-added and are directly linked to major corporate decisions, product development and investment strategies. If a society is to attract and keep the activities that drive these corporations, it needs to take steps to participate actively in their ownership and control and to have a skilled workforce that can fill these strategic positions.

However, the increasing importance of small production units both in creating new jobs and in protecting existing ones indicates the limitations of any approach to economic policy centred exclusively on large-scale production. This observation is especially crucial for Quebec, where small business plays a preponderant role in the economy.

Cities, Towns and Regions: The Pillars of Quebec's Development

The industrial policies that make up an economic strategy emphasizing job creation through small business cannot simply be miniature replicas of those directed towards large projects. There are two fundamental ingredients of such a strategy: the economic initiative of the population and the occupational skills of the workers in a country and its regions.

When a society places primary emphasis on the proliferation and growth of small production units to provide economic growth and job creation, its capacity to encourage different forms of economic initiative in its population becomes a determining factor in its economic performance. Initiatives of this sort need fertile ground if they are to succeed. Since small businesses cannot, as a general rule, count on significant economies of scale in the early stages of their existence, they need advantages other than those that come from very large production runs.

It is usually when small businesses become linked to closely knit networks of suppliers and customers that they are most successful in turning their size to advantage. When they can cultivate special relationships with one another and pool their resources and expertise to adjust quickly to changing market conditions, they can develop innovative products to exploit profitable niches in both domestic and international markets.

It is increasingly important to be able to benefit from complementary economic activities and comparative advantage directly attributable to geographical proximity. In this light, it is worth taking a new look at the role of cities, towns and regions in economic development. We can now see more clearly that over the medium and long term, encouraging local initiative is a more significant determining factor in a region's development than building megaprojects based on foreign investment, which often have no relation to the local economic fabric. Indeed, it is most often in cities, towns and regions that have been able to develop links among their producers that megaprojects have had the most beneficial effects, as it is there that subcontracting relationships have grown up with locally established small and medium-sized production units.

In this context, new kinds of economic policy have begun to appear over the last few decades. These new approaches are increasingly based on getting socioeconomic actors to work together, on creating and strengthening links between business and cities, towns and regions, and on developing and implementing local or regional economic development strategies. The chief lesson of these approaches is that the dynamism of cities, towns and regions and their capacity to mobilize their resources for shared projects are the foundation of a society's economic strength.

To mobilize in this way and to use their strengths to best advantage, cities, towns and regions must be endowed with the autonomy and the resources they need. Another part of the adjustment effort that

Quebec must undertake should be the establishment of an institutional and political framework that will allow regions to take charge of their development and encourage economic initiative among their people.

Social Solidarity: A Condition for Development

Thus, while one trend has led national economies to become more integrated with one another, another has led towards stronger economic cohesion in cities, towns and regions. In response to these apparently opposite trends, governments have, on the one hand, increasingly delegated responsibilities to new international institutions and, on the other, decentralized some of their powers to local bodies. This rearrangement of economic space and political responsibility has radically changed our perception of the role of government in modern societies. Nor has rethinking the role of government been limited to the economic sphere: the social mission of government has been affected as well.

In the postwar period, the governments of developed countries succeeded in reconciling the goal of economic growth with that of social justice. Redistribution of wealth through universal social programs had the effect of stimulating demand in periods of economic slowdown, with a positive impact on the level of production and — in the early postwar years — employment as well. These policies brought about sustained growth for more than three decades, interrupted only by temporary recessions. The result was the emergence of the first mass consumer societies in human history.

But the two oil shocks of the 1970s, followed by two severe recessions in the early 1980s and the early 1990s, showed that this model of economic management had reached its limit. The fiscal and financial crisis that governments face is one of the most conspicuous manifestations of this change. The universal social programs and sophisticated networks of public services put into place during the years of prosperity have drained an increasing proportion of governments' resources. The numbers of people dependent on these programs grow while the middle class, from which governments obtain the largest part of their revenues, erodes.

This process has led to a political impasse in developed countries, which has taken the form of widespread questioning of the welfare state and the dramatic rise of neoconservative ideology. A number of governments endorsed the withdrawal of the state from some of the fields it occupied during the years of prosperity and opted to give free play to market forces rather than intervene to redistribute wealth to the same degree as in the past.

It was not long before the consequences of such policies were felt. Increasing inequality became the most troubling economic and social phenomenon of the 1980s, and market forces, left to themselves, quickly proved powerless to stop it. Formerly prosperous towns and regions sank into structural decline. as their populations shifted to large centres. Even in the most dynamic metropolitan areas, large pockets of poverty appeared, transforming communities into ghettos which are isolated from one another and unable to agree on an alternative vision of their future or mobilize their energies to find a common solution to their problems.

The new social, cultural and economic rifts resulting from these trends can now be seen in virtually all developed societies, Quebec among them. Sometimes pitting dynamic regions against declining ones, sometimes pitting the privileged against the marginalized, these rifts impose a heavy burden on our political institutions, which have proved increasingly unable to mobilize the resources of the societies they represent.

From this perspective, reaffirming our goals of social justice and equality of opportunity is especially urgent. We need to resist the increasing inequalities in our society and the increasing challenges to social solidarity. The limitations of the solutions worked out during the years of prosperity, based essentially on the establishment of universal social programs and public services, have no doubt become clear. But it will only make things worse if governments sit on the sidelines while whole sectors of our economy are radically restructured. Instead, governments have to work out policies that are better adapted to the new realities, develop more flexible ways of intervening and rethink their methods of redistributing wealth.

A Cultural Plan

While the trend towards globalization of the economy has been taking shape, equally significant changes have been occurring in the cultural sphere. Both the content of national cultures and the values that underlie our ways of living together have been profoundly disturbed.

Today, information circulates throughout the world through globalized media networks. All sorts of issues and events that used to be confined to a specific society are now part of a media universe that completely cuts through national cultures. Far from slowing down, this trend continues to gather speed as existing media become more widespread (through such innovations as satellite television) and new media appear. However, while we can follow the twists and turns of faraway conflicts as they happen, we are too often unaware of events that affect our own region, and we are even more ignorant of those affecting other regions within our society. Paradoxically, the globalization of the media emphasizes the fragility of the information system on which the cohesion of national cultures depends.

Another new development is the rise of international marketing strategies for cultural products. The various creative disciplines in the cultural and artistic sphere have also entered the global era. Few areas of human creativity have escaped the globalization of cultural issues and trends. These tendencies can be seen in the interpretive or the plastic arts, in architecture or literature, in the physical or social sciences. The underlying logic through which research is carried out, knowledge is produced, products are distributed and fashions and trends are validated is increasingly a transnational one. National cultures cannot passively submit to these influences and absorb them without becoming impoverished and homogenized. They have to participate in these new currents and be enriched by them without renouncing the basis of their own identity.

The massive international migration of the last few decades is yet another factor contributing to cultural globalization. In this period, millions of international migrants and people from rural areas have swelled the populations of large urban centres. In the contemporary city, vast new human and social realities are daily being built. People with increasingly diverse backgrounds and cultural attitudes need to learn to live together, reconcile their values and aspirations, and develop a shared vision of their future. For better or for worse, in its successes and its failures, the modern city has become a melting pot in which a new and profoundly urban culture marked with the stamp of diversity and change is being forged.

While national cultures are challenged by all these developments, they still need to play a fundamental role in guiding the development of contemporary societies. Our culture is defined by a shared language, a shared history and heritage, and shared values and institutions. It is through our culture that we shape our life together, our forms of solidarity and our common projects. As globalization transforms national cultures, it will bring new elements that can enrich them. At the same time, however, it will change those elements that unite our societies and raise issues that are central for all peoples.

From now on, national realities will have to be expressed in this global context. It was the secretary general of the United Nations, Boutros Boutros-Ghali, who best described the new role of nations in a speech on nationalism and globalization delivered in Montreal on May 24, 1992:

> Each individual needs an intermediary between the universe, which transcends him, and his solitary state — if only because he needs an initial language in order to understand and decode the outside world. He needs firm allegiances, and a set of cultural references, in a word, an "access code" to the world. It is this set of needs that are met by nation-States, which transcend the immediate allegiances of the family, the clan and the village. A nation is a common "will to live" which constitutes a first step towards the universal, towards the universal civilization.

Thus, the globalization of markets has deep cultural implications. It has been said that from now on our standard of living will depend on the skills of our population. If we want to maintain the social levels we have achieved, we will need to make sure that we produce high-quality, innovative goods and services that can compete with those from countries that have put their money on knowhow, creativity and the ability of their workers to adapt to a changing environment. We can achieve these qualities only through an overall cultural plan that can mobilize our whole population.

The foundations of such a plan are accessible, high-quality education, individual creativity, and the solidarity, responsibility and autonomy of local communities. Today, an economic strategy for our society cannot be viable and social justice cannot be lasting without a genuine Quebec cultural plan based on values such as these. In light of the nature and requirements of a plan of this sort, sovereignty is the most appropriate political framework for implementing it.

A Society that Fulfills Our Aspirations

Sovereignty will give Quebec the capacity to take action and will open up new prospects for its people's progress. Freed from the federal yoke, Quebec will be able to meet the challenge of being a dynamic society integrated into a very demanding international environment. Relying on our own strengths and assets and endowed with the instruments we need, we will achieve that goal.

[However, accession to full political sovereignty is not an end in itself. Rather, it is the political key to Quebec's progress.] With full decision-making powers and control over the levers of development, Quebec will be in a better position to guarantee improvement in all facets of the social life of its population. In short, sovereignty is an essential precondition to implementing a genuine *projet de société*, an authentic Quebec social plan.

A Plan Centred on Jobs

Jobs are at the heart of this plan. The goal of job creation is an almost brutal necessity. All developed societies are taking a long time to recover from the world recession and are struggling with its effects, but Quebec's position is especially unenviable in that unemployment here has reached a level that is intolerable in economic terms and even more so in human terms. Furthermore, the reality hidden behind the official figures is that not only has employment failed to grow but the quality of the jobs available has also dropped. The proportion of total employment consisting of unstable part-time jobs has increased substantially.

This level of unemployment puts almost unbearable pressure on the financing of our social programs. Today, for each Quebecer who benefits from one of the three major income support programs — social assistance, unemployment insurance and the guaranteed income supplement — there are only two working Quebecers who contribute to the financing of these programs. These conditions represent a threat to the ties of solidarity that unite us.

Like other societies not so different from our own, Quebec can rebuild and strengthen its networks of solidarity and move towards full employment by making job creation the central objective, even the obsession, of its economic development strategy. To reach this point, however, we first need the means to fulfil our ambitions.

Sovereignty will provide us with the conditions in which full employment can be achieved because it will, at long last, make possible reaching the crucial goal of coherence in our policies relating to economic development — job training policies, fiscal and budgetary policies, industrial and agricultural policies, regional development policies.

Human Resources

It has become a truism: the future belongs primarily to societies that can develop the potential of their human resources. No longer can we base our development on our natural resources alone. Natural resources still have a role to play, but more than ever we have to develop our skills. This means that we should make education a social priority, set ambitious goals and take action to fulfil them. If Quebec is to have a true *projet de société*, a plan for education must be its inspiration and foundation.

In the last few years, Quebec society has changed, the fabric of the family has been altered, and student populations and educational options have become more diverse. The new economic context and technological change also put considerable pressure on the education system. From kindergarten to university, our education system needs to adjust to these new realities without losing sight of its primary mission: the development of the whole person.

Hence, Quebec should take the necessary steps to guarantee that all its young people receive a solid basic education. First and foremost, this means sufficient mastery of language, the cornerstone of any occupational training. Quebec's efforts in basic education should aim at making it possible for all students to obtain a secondary school diploma, which today represents the minimum educational requirement in advanced societies.

In this regard, Quebec's school dropout rate of more than 35 per cent is nothing short of a tragedy. To solve the school dropout problem, schools need to motivate students, offer them a welcoming environment and provide them with personalized guidance that leads them towards vocational training and the acquisition of knowledge. Other elements that make for successful schools and students include improved teacher training and greater involvement by those who are on education's front lines — parents as well as teachers and other school employees. Education cannot be the same in all parts of Quebec and has to respond to the needs of different socioeconomic environments. There should be real autonomy at the local level in making choices and developing instruments to respond to specific situations and diverse learning needs.

Once improved basic general education is in place, we will be able to encourage more young people to pursue postsecondary studies. In colleges and universities, we need to create conditions in which more people continue their education and go on to graduate. Quebec is far from having caught up in this regard, especially in some scientific and technical fields. We need more researchers — more people with masters' degrees and doctorates.

A strategy whose goal is full employment must be based on a sustained effort to train our workforce. In this context, occupational training programs play a crucial role in enabling us to create high-quality jobs that Quebecers can fill. The advantages of this branch of education have to be demonstrated to young people, who have tended to stay away from it in the last few years. In a variety of sectors that generate economic development, Quebec has a shortage of skilled workers. Why does Quebec have only 14,000 young people registered in the occupational training courses offered by school boards, as compared with 100,000 fifteen years ago? How can we tolerate this situation? It is imperative that business be able to count on an adequate supply of skilled workers who can innovate, adjust and take advantage of technological change.

As people will now be called on to move from job to job and deal with changing job specifications in the course of their working lives, they should have continuing access to retraining and upgrading programs. This is an area where we need a real turnaround, both in the school system and in business. Schools will have to do better by becoming more closely linked with the job market. Business will have to do more by increasing its investment in the training of its workers. Thus, a major change in our traditions and our way of doing things is essential in this area. In particular, we need to set up an apprenticeship system in which periods of study alternate with periods of work.

Job training is undoubtedly one of the sectors where the ineffectiveness and bankruptcy of Canadian federalism can be seen most clearly. A jumble of parallel federal and provincial programs creates a labyrinth of procedures, measures and forms in which workers, job seekers and companies get lost. Job training is recognized as one of the most strategic elements of economic development and was at the heart of the proposals in the Charlottetown Accord. Nevertheless, Quebec and federal ministers have proved incapable of renegotiating a federal-provincial agreement that expired at the end of March 1992 and that everyone recognized as inadequate. Sovereignty will make it possible to put an end to costly duplication, simplify programs and set up a "one-stop shopping" system for workers and job seekers in each region.

Business

Quebec businesses are facing increasing competition in ever more extensive markets. The key to their productivity and competitiveness lies in the quality of their human resources and their capacity to adapt to accelerating scientific and technological innovation and change. We will achieve this capacity for innovation only with an unprecedented effort in research and development. Quebec devotes only 1.5 per cent of its gross domestic product to R&D, one of the lowest figures in the western world. It is also a victim of clear discrimination in the allocation of federal R&D funds. In 1990, only 18.8 per cent of federal spending on R&D went to Quebec, while more than 50 per cent went to Ontario.

Once Quebec has the necessary instruments, all of Quebec society will have to be mobilized in the area of R&D. This mobilization will enlist business, universities, research centres and institutes and government laboratories in a concerted effort. Better synergy among all the partners will need to be established. The government will have to offer concrete support to initiatives to increase our R&D

potential, and companies, which will reap substantial dividends, will have to become involved in a variety of ways.

Sovereignty will also provide a framework in which Quebec's own particular model of economic development can flourish. This model is based on convergence and interaction among private, public, joint and cooperative institutions. There is no question of the Quebec government's adopting an indifferent or hands-off attitude. In light of the international context and the scale of our economy, it will need to play a dynamic role in encouraging partnership among different social and economic stakeholders as well as investment and entrepreneurship.

Partnership has already produced results, but we should go a lot further. For a full employment policy to work, it is essential for all stakeholders in employment — government, business, the cooperative movement, trade unions, community groups and educational institutions — to participate and work together. To achieve this, we will need to establish mechanisms that are both flexible and effective. Here public authorities have the role of orchestra conductor or catalyst: they ensure that cohesion and solidarity among economic stakeholders work to best advantage.

Experiments with partnership and cooperation should also take place within companies, in the workplace. A firm can only benefit from the active involvement of its employees in decisions regarding the organization of work and production methods.

Models of worker participation in the ownership and management of companies will also be encouraged.

Sovereignty will provide Quebec with the array of fiscal and financial instruments it needs to carry out a coherent industrial development strategy. It therefore will inevitably have a positive effect on many elements of Quebec's industrial development, such as the growth of a network of Quebec suppliers or the reinvestment of profits in R&D. We should also take steps to ensure that Quebec companies can count on increased availability of risk capital through financial intermediaries.

As a province, Quebec has developed historically within the Canadian common market — an artificial market in many respects given its geographical constraints. As a sovereign state, it will benefit from the North American economic space now taking shape. Our economy will remain largely outward looking, and Quebec companies should be on an equal footing as they take on the challenge of penetrating foreign markets.

Quebec's Regions

Balanced development of Quebec's regions is another important element in full employment. A number of regions, especially those whose development has traditionally been based on natural resources, have undergone an alarming economic decline. Many rural communities have been ravaged by unemployment and have to deal with out-migration and an aging population. The economic development of each region has to be rooted in that region's particular reality. Development strategies and plans should be conceived and created in the regions themselves, on the basis of their needs and assets. It is first and foremost at the regional level that economic partners can and should work together to maintain and create jobs.

Competition and fruitless quarrels between the federal and Quebec governments have done the regions a great deal of harm. Unfortunately, the financing of regional projects is all too often blocked by the inertia that results from bureaucratic rivalry. In addition, in the agricultural sector, which is a significant component of the economy in a number of regions, Quebec producers have often been ill served by federal programs. Sovereignty will make it possible to put an end to duplication and overlap in agricultural and regional development policies and reorient these policies on the basis of our own priorities.

But that will not be enough. For one thing, government programs need to be recast and made more flexible to respond to specific local situations. What is good for the Abitibi region is not necessarily good for the Gaspé region or the Saint-Maurice Valley. For another, regions should have the necessary tools and suitable resources to realize their wish to take charge of their own economic development by creating local and regional partnerships, setting development goals and establishing instruments to carry them out. Thus, firm support for regional development funds will provide local and regional communities with the resources they need to finance projects that respect their priorities.

The difficulties that resource regions are undergoing make it a priority to devote attention to diversifying their economic activities. Tangible recognition should also be given to the special role of Montreal and its metropolitan area in generating economic development. And Quebec City should be endowed with all the attributes of a genuine political and administrative capital.

Once the Quebec government recovers substantial fiscal resources and broadens its responsibilities, it will finally be able to take the decisive action needed to achieve real decentralization of powers to regions and local communities.

Bringing revenues and powers back to Quebec will make it possible to undertake a major reform of our administrative and decision-making system. Our aim should be to bring services closer to citizens by giving them input into the way services are dispensed. We will thus be able to entrust the management of public services and the administration of government programs to the institutions that can perform these tasks most effectively. With real powers and decision-making instruments, regions will be able to act on economic development and local communities will be in a better position to identify their own needs and choose the most appropriate way of responding to them.

We would be missing the point if we were to impose predetermined structures from on high. But one thing is certain: this effort to redefine the way administrative functions are carried out and reorganize decision-making centres will result in more responsibilities being exercised by the municipalities, the urban communities, and the regional county municipalities.

Sustainable Development

The deep ecological crisis worldwide has confronted us with urgent choices. Quebec should begin now to commit itself to a path of sustainable development. To this end, Quebec's model of economic development will be directed towards protecting the environment, preserving ecological balance and renewing and conserving resources.

To achieve this, it is essential to go further than fighting pollution in all its forms. The fight against pollution is necessary, of course, and should be intensified so that we can return to a healthy environment and restore our natural surroundings. Industrial and other polluters should assume their responsibilities in this regard. But ecological damage also needs to be eliminated at its source, and this means modifying our ways of both producing and consuming. The dissipation and waste of resources should be stopped and integrated land management methods should be introduced. We also need to institute a serious policy of recovering and recycling domestic, industrial and agricultural waste. In the energy sector, we need to achieve greater efficiency and give priority to renewable, nonpolluting sources of energy.

Quebec has waited too long to act on environmental concerns. From now on, we should try to be among the leaders in the vital task of protecting ecosystems. A sovereign Quebec should also contribute to the resolution of ecological problems that have an international dimension. When we talk about cross-border pollution with our neighbours, our discussions will be all the more fruitful if they are based on exemplary behaviour within our own territory.

Social Solidarity

Quebec's development should be based on principles of justice, equity and solidarity. Quebec is currently suffering from severe social ills. To be sure, we can point to substantial achievements in making adequate education and health services available to everyone. We have established a social safety net for people who are unemployed or sick. We have taken steps to provide older people with a decent retirement. But this is no longer enough.

A growing proportion of the population is now excluded from the prosperity of our society. Almost a million young people and adults in Quebec are trapped in structural poverty and all the problems that go along with it. Increasingly, our social programs are proving powerless to deal with this problem, which is concentrated in areas whose boundaries are ever more clearly marked: urban neighbourhoods suffering from deindustrialization and declining rural regions. This is an intolerable social cleavage. Repairing the ties that unite us and recreating a society whose different components live together in solidarity represent difficult and exciting challenges for a sovereign Quebec.

Equality of Opportunity

The goal of genuine equality of opportunity is the fundamental inspiration of our *projet de société*. This sense of equality should be a reality very early in life, during the crucial period of childhood. There is a high probability that a child who lives in poverty will do poorly in school, drop out, fall into delinquency and face a dead end. We need to begin intervening in early childhood to provide everyone with an equal chance at having the best possible start in life. This means offering adequate support to families, extending and improving child care services, and establishing early stimulation and learning programs. Quebec can and should do better in all these areas, for the seeds of future success are planted in early childhood.

Quebec also needs to provide youth with a real place in society. Today's young people enter a more complex, more competitive and less welcoming world than previous generations. Adult society often seems closed to their aspirations and real needs. Above all, providing youth with a place in society means offering them a solid general education that will be supplemented with postsecondary studies or vocational training.

Although Quebec has been taking steps to democratize the education system for thirty years, young people still do not have equal access to education. Since students from disadvantaged backgrounds are more likely to drop out, programs to deal with this problem should be targeted to client groups that are most severely affected by it. In particular, there is still significant inequality of access to university education. It is our firm intention to maintain the principle of free education at the CEGEP (community college and pre-university) level, and we also need to establish financial support mechanisms that will encourage young people to undertake and complete advanced studies. The mammoth education drive that Quebec should be inspired to undertake will also include adult education, as there are still too many adults who are illiterate or lack adequate basic skills.

Providing a place for young people also means making it possible for them to have access to high-quality jobs. We should ease their transition to the labour market, especially by providing practical training, and encourage their initiatives. A society that has a future will be one that encourages its young people to be enterprising, innovative and successful, one that channels their dynamism, creativity and potential. We need to bridge the generation gap and rebuild social solidarity for the sake of our youth.

Equality of Women and Men

Quebec should also vigorously promote equality of opportunity between women and men. Despite the progress that has been made, women are still a long way from attaining the status that is their due or enjoying equal conditions in most areas of social life. More women live in poverty. Women who work are generally paid less than men. Women still bear the primary burden of parental responsibility and are clearly underrepresented in circles of economic and political power. Correcting this situation will require a multipronged approach: removing the constraints that discourage young women from choosing the careers of the future, providing training that will help women get jobs, instituting genuine pay equity, and making it possible for women to reconcile family and career through appropriate support measures.

It should be pointed out that our current political system disadvantages women in particular. Tax provisions regarding spouses and children are incoherent, and there is duplication in federal and provincial job training and family support programs. Sovereignty will make it possible to recast programs — tax provisions, family support payments, maternity leave — and centralize them in Quebec so that an effective, coherent family policy can be established.

Participation in the Wealth of Society

Quebec will make a firm commitment to the struggle against poverty. The primary causes of poverty are unemployment and inadequate education. Poverty in turn causes people to become dependent, devalued and marginalized and leads to serious disparities in health, life expectancy and children's educational attainment. Efforts should of course be made to mitigate the effects of poverty through an income support program, special measures targeted at disadvantaged children and guaranteed access to suitable and affordable housing. But here too it is necessary to address the source of the problems. It is possible to break the vicious cycle of poverty and dependency by enhancing the employability of people who are trapped in it. Adequate occupational training and retraining programs can bring people back into the workforce.

We must end the jumble that characterizes the area of income security. Here as elsewhere, there is one government too many. Eliminating the unnecessary government will put Quebec in a position to harmonize social assistance, unemployment insurance and job training programs under the overall heading of a work access policy. By harmonizing its tax code with the various programs of direct support to individuals and households, Quebec will also be able to provide everyone with a guaranteed minimum income while encouraging people's active involvement in improving their own living conditions.

In the area of health, continuing to offer free and universal services to Quebec's population is a token of the essential solidarity that we need to maintain. There would be no question of ending public financing of our system of health and social services, whose quality is widely acknowledged. We do need a concerted effort to reduce the considerable gaps in health and life expectancy among different sectors of the population.

Our aims should also include: humanizing services to a greater extent; giving higher priority to small units such as CLSCs (community health and social service centres), which are in a better position to adjust their practices to the particular characteristics of their environment and to act effectively on the front lines; and encouraging the involvement of practitioners and users through genuine decentralization of decision-making powers.

Banking on Community Action

Quebec's experience has taught us that the welfare state cannot solve all social problems. Collectively, we have invested substantial resources in a variety of services and a multitude of assistance and support programs to provide a better life for Quebec's population, but the results have not come close to our expectations. Traditional mechanisms for redistributing wealth have their limits, and highly unequal distribution of wealth persists. A growing number of people fall through the cracks in our social safety net. Standardized government programs have had their day. Quebec will need to be more flexible in its practices and adjust its ways of intervening to the different realities of diverse social environments.

To achieve our social justice objectives, we will also need to bank on community action. Many groups of people are putting their energies together and giving themselves the tools to solve their problems and improve their lot. The common interest on which such groups are based could be mutual assistance, housing or health; prevention of violence, education or recreation; economic development or jobs. This plethora of groups is a sign of dynamism and a will to change things. They should have freedom of action and the resources they need for their initiatives to succeed.

This does not mean that the government should abandon its responsibilities on the pretext of budget rationalization. On the contrary, it should support the activities of these groups, which are often in a much better position to meet citizens' needs than large bureaucratic institutions. Quebec should encourage local communities to organize.

A Dynamic Culture

Culture binds people together — it is the expression of their feeling of belonging to a collectivity. It is embodied in our particular ways of living, thinking and creating. In the special context of North America, Quebec culture constantly needs to assert itself. It needs to encourage creativity and the expression of its originality, while enriching itself by integrating contributions from outside. These are the conditions of its dynamism and indeed of its survival.

Sovereignty will provide a framework and mechanisms through which Quebec culture can be both internally cohesive and externally influential. It will give Quebec control over all the instruments it needs to develop its cultural identity. The Quebec government will then be able to invest the money brought back from Ottawa to support artists and cultural groups on the basis of our society's priorities and needs.

Because radio and television occupy such a central place in the production and distribution of cultural works, a communications policy will be an integral part of Quebec's overall cultural policy. Faced with the powerful American cultural machine and the limited size of our own market, Quebec culture must be able to depend on active public support. The government of a sovereign Quebec should continue to assume the responsibilities incumbent on it as the government of the only majority Francophone society on the continent.

The French language is the cornerstone of Quebec's cultural identity. It is and will remain the official language of Quebec. It is and will remain the preferred instrument for integrating newcomers into Quebec society. However, a Quebec that wants to be open to the world needs to encourage its citizens to learn other languages, especially English.

First and foremost, cultural dynamism is based on the vitality and potential of our artists and creative people. The goal of Quebec cultural policy should be to establish conditions that encourage artistic creation, distribution of the works of our creative people, and citizens' access to culture from both Quebec and elsewhere. This means that support for culture should be one of the essential functions of government, on the same level as support for economic development. Whatever form this support takes should be characterized by respect for freedom and diversity of expression. In this light, the funds devoted to cultural support programs should be managed by arm's-length granting agencies. In addition, businesses and municipalities should be encouraged to invest more and become more involved in the cultural sector.

A fundamental objective of any cultural policy should be to allow as many citizens as possible to have access to expressions of culture. Accessibility is a condition of cultural development and the quality of life of a society, and it cannot be achieved without the existence of an adequate cultural infrastructure. The serious deficiencies in the cultural infrastructure of many regions should be quickly alleviated by bringing together regional cultural agencies and local authorities to identify their needs and priorities.

Schools can do their part by helping students to develop a taste for culture and by encouraging more people to undertake careers in the arts. We should also devote more effort to restoring our historic architecture and to other aspects of our heritage. This legacy represents a window on our past and can help stimulate tourism as well.

The Quebec government has an important role to play in promoting the international distribution of Quebec culture, especially by being actively involved in the Francophone world and stepping up its exchanges with Francophone countries.

Culture cannot be monolithic, in Quebec or anywhere else. In a world where all kinds of exchanges take place, culture is naturally subject to the play of outside influences. It partially assimilates these influences and is transformed by them. To the degree that Quebec society includes citizens of a variety of ethnic origins and cultural traditions, their contribution is part of the source material of its culture. Quebec should recognize the richness of the cultural baggage that people who have chosen to live here bring with them.

A Pluralist Society

The Anglophone community has contributed greatly to the development of Quebec in every field of activity. Indeed, when Quebec's political status is clarified, a foundation will be laid for Francophone and Anglophone Quebecers to live together more harmoniously and fruitfully. For a Quebec that is open to the outside and has close relations with its North American neighbours, it is a significant advantage to have a dynamic Anglophone community. The individual rights of Quebec Anglophones will be guaranteed and the community will be able to continue to count on a secure network of educational, social and cultural institutions that can maintain its vitality.

No society is free of xenophobic behaviour or racist incidents. Quebec should be firmly committed to fighting all forms of discrimination that can affect members of cultural communities, and especially visible minorities. The full participation of citizens of all origins in Quebec's development should be based on a determination to ensure equal economic and social as well as political rights.

Quebec's accession to sovereignty will make it possible to clarify the often uncomfortable situation of many new Quebecers who maintain a feeling of dual allegiance to Quebec and Canada. Candidates for immigration to Quebec will be making the conscious choice of a staunchly French-speaking society. Quebec's traditions as a society that has welcomed immigrants will be an advantage in making it easier for newcomers to integrate harmoniously in terms of language, social relations and economic life. Clearly, newcomers will be invited to share some values common to Quebec society; at the same time, it will be important to help all people in Quebec become more sensitive to the realities of intercultural relations. To encourage immigrants to settle in all parts of Quebec, mechanisms should be provided to receive them so that they can contribute to the development of Quebec's regions. In short, a major aspect of Quebec's *projet de société* consists of being open to immigration and integrating cultural communities.

Aboriginal people will have a special place in a sovereign Quebec since they were the first inhabitants. They will have the tools they need to preserve their traditions and affirm their cultures. In line with the National Assembly's 1985 resolution declaring aboriginal communities to be distinct nations, autonomous aboriginal governments will be the cornerstone of their new social contract with the Quebec nation and their participation in Quebec's development.

Sovereignty: A Clear and Coherent Plan

The referendum of October 26, 1992 marked the end of a five-year journey through the constitutional maze. From the point of view of the movement to make Quebec a sovereign state, this period turned out to be a very productive one.

The sustained and sometimes dramatic growth in popular support for sovereignty was one clear expression of the period's fertility. Just as remarkable, however, was the extraordinary number of reflections, debates, reports, position papers and technical clarifications through which all aspects of sovereignty were formulated more explicitly than ever before. New clarity has been achieved on issues as diverse as currency, territorial integrity and minority rights.

It is significant that this process involved all of Quebec society, especially through the work of the Commission on the Political and Constitutional Future of Quebec (the Bélanger-Campeau Commission) in 1990-91. Since the commission did not operate in an exclusively sovereignist perspective, its deliberations provided an opportunity to compare sovereignty with the alternative proposal of renewed federalism, making this initiative an extremely fruitful one.

The Bélanger-Campeau Commission was one of two exceptional forums that provided an opportunity for people to express themselves in oral testimony and written briefs, for experts to discuss and clarify technical questions, and for elected representatives to draw conclusions and elements of consensus bearing on Quebec's political future. However, the report of the Bélanger-Campeau Commission, the studies carried out by its secretariat, and the draft report of the Quebec National Assembly committee that studied questions relating to Quebec's accession to sovereignty have received limited distribution. It is worth taking another look at the major conclusions of these forums to help clarify and define some of the fundamental elements involved in making Quebec a sovereign state.

The Definition of Sovereignty

For the first time, a consensus has been reached on the definition of sovereignty. This definition is the one that the Quebec government used in 1979 in the white paper it issued to lay the basis for the 1980 referendum. It also forms part of the current program of the Parti Québécois. The Bélanger-Campeau Commission endorsed it as well. And finally, the Quebec National Assembly adopted this definition by including it in Bill 150, its 1991 legislation providing for a referendum on sovereignty by October 26, 1992, unless the federal government developed a proposal that could be put to the people instead.

The sovereignty of Quebec means that

- all taxes imposed in Quebec are collected by the Quebec government or authorities dependent on it;
- all laws that apply to Quebec citizens on Quebec soil emanate from the Quebec National Assembly;
- all international treaties, conventions and agreements are negotiated by representatives of the Quebec government and ratified by the Quebec National Assembly.

These three elements — taxes, legislation and treaties — encompass all government activity internally and internationally. Given the way today's world is organized, no state can afford to become isolated or withdrawn. In acquiring complete freedom of action, Quebec will also assume responsibility for conducting its relations with other members of the international community. Of primary importance will be relations with Canada. Quebec should ensure that the Canadian economic space is maintained. It can also pool a portion of its powers in any sector where the interests of two or more countries are involved. Quebec will look for these paths to the future wherever it is in its interest to do so.

Accession to Sovereignty

The Parti Québécois defined the process of acceding to sovereignty at its conventions in November 1988 and January 1991. It specified the major steps it will take to achieve the sovereignty of Quebec in the event that it is called on to form a government. These are the steps:

* From now until the time that it forms the next government, the Parti Québécois will promote Quebec sovereignty by concretely demonstrating its advantages.
* Once elected, a Parti Québécois government will

    a) submit to the National Assembly for adoption a solemn declaration stating Quebec's wish to accede to full sovereignty;

    b) following discussions with the federal government, proceed to fulfil its responsibility and its mandate to establish the timetable and modalities for transferring powers and determine the rules for dividing Canada's assets and debts;

    c) submit to the National Assembly for adoption legislation instituting a constitutional commission whose terms of reference would be to draw up a proposed constitution for a sovereign Quebec.

- As quickly as possible, the government will ask the population, through a referendum, to speak on the sovereignty of Quebec and the constitutional mechanisms that would make the exercise of that sovereignty possible. This referendum will be the act that will bring into being a sovereign Quebec.
- The Quebec government will also propose mutually advantageous forms of economic association to the federal government. These proposals will include the institution of joint bodies, established through treaties, to manage the economic relationship between Canada and Quebec.

It is our intention to ensure that accession to sovereignty takes place in as democratic a framework as possible. Here we will specify, as far as we can, the steps and conditions that will lead to a sovereign Quebec.

The Quebec Constitution

The Constitution of Quebec will be the supreme law of the land. It will define the institutions through which the people of Quebec choose to govern themselves, and it will guarantee all the fundamental rights and freedoms of Quebec citizens. It is only by giving itself a constitution that Quebec can become sovereign.

To start with, the constitution needs to recognize the sovereignty of the people and establish the bodies that will exercise state power in its name. For an initial period at least, it would appear to be in Quebec's interest essentially to hold over its existing institutions and make only those modifications that are immediately required by the change in its political status.

This means that the existing system of executive and legislative authority would be maintained. The only change would be the replacement of the lieutenant-governor, whose responsibilities could be exercised by a ceremonial head of state elected by a majority of members of the National Assembly. The National Assembly itself could be maintained in its present form, as the new powers it would obtain would not require it to change the way it functions.

Changes to the judicial system would involve the establishment of a Supreme Court of Quebec and the incorporation into the Quebec judicial structure of a number of courts that now operate under federal legislation. Just as federal civil servants will be integrated into the Quebec civil service, places can be found for federally appointed judges within Quebec courts — on condition, of course, of their allegiance to the new constitution.

It will also be a function of the constitution to lay out Quebecers' rights and freedoms. To this end, the Quebec Charter of Rights and Freedoms will be entrenched in the constitution.

The constitution should include new and clear guarantees of the rights of the Anglophone minority. Quebec owes much to Quebecers of English culture, and it should act to ensure that the constitution expresses and guarantees their fundamental and acquired rights in the best possible fashion.

In the same way, the rights of aboriginal peoples will be preserved. The Constitution of Quebec should include the same guarantees of ancestral and treaty rights now offered by the Constitution of Canada. In addition, in the spirit of the National Assembly's 1985 decision to recognize aboriginal peoples as distinct nations, the constitution will provide explicit recognition of their right to autonomous governments and protection for agreements that would put this autonomy into practice in a context of respect for Quebec's territorial integrity.

The constitution also needs to include an amending formula. In addition to these provisions, temporary measures will be taken to allow for Quebec's transition from provincial status to the status of a sovereign state, especially with regard to the continuity of laws and institutions.

This transitional constitution will be prepared by the constitutional commission that a Parti Québécois government will establish after being elected. It could also be within the commission's terms of reference to study more thorough changes to Quebec's institutions. Should such changes be considered desirable, they could then be adopted after Quebec became sovereign.

Quebec Citizenship

Every state determines who its citizens are — to which people it will accord nationality or citizenship. Quebec citizenship will be automatically granted to all Canadian citizens domiciled in Quebec at the moment of Quebec's accession to sovereignty, and from that time on, to all children born to Quebec parents inside or outside Quebec territory. All Canadian citizens born in Quebec but domiciled elsewhere in Canada or outside Canada at the time of accession to sovereignty because of the position they occupy — students, missionaries, businesspeople, members of the armed forces, civil servants, et cetera — will also become Quebec citizens. To facilitate its nationals' relations with other countries, Quebec will issue a passport identifying its bearer as possessing Quebec nationality.

Landed immigrants will be able to obtain Quebec citizenship once the waiting period under Canadian legislation in force at the time of accession to sovereignty has elapsed. From then on, Quebec will exercise full powers over immigration. With respect to refugees, Quebec will sign the 1951 Convention relating to the Status of Refugees and its protocol and the 1966 International Convention on Civil and Political Rights and its protocol, which are the most important multilateral agreements in this regard.

Quebec intends to grant Quebec citizenship automatically, with no waiting period, to any Canadian citizen who decides to become domiciled in Quebec. It will propose to the government of Canada that a reciprocal agreement be concluded in this regard so that any Quebec citizen who settles in Canada can immediately become a Canadian citizen. The two countries could also agree not to establish immigration quotas affecting each other's nationals so that the advantages of the free movement of people prevailing before Quebec's accession to sovereignty would be maintained.

It will, of course, be Canada's responsibility to take any decisions it considers appropriate with regard to Canadian citizenship. It could, for example, decide to maintain Canadian citizenship for any Canadian citizen residing in Quebec before Quebec's accession to sovereignty, or for any such person who requests it. Like current Canadian legislation, Quebec citizenship legislation will recognize the possibility of its nationals' holding dual citizenship.

Territory

What will be the borders of a sovereign Quebec? The work of the National Assembly's committee on questions relating to sovereignty has made it possible to clarify questions surrounding the issue of territory.

First of all, before Quebec becomes sovereign, under the provisions of the Canadian constitution, its borders cannot be changed without its consent. After it becomes sovereign, the framework for questions of its territorial integrity will be international law.

Thus, when Quebec becomes sovereign, its borders will be the borders of the current province of Quebec. Some people have maintained that the lands transferred to Quebec under federal legislation in 1898 and 1912, which extended its territory to the shores of Hudson Bay, Hudson Strait and Ungava Bay, could then be cut off from Quebec. The committee submitted this question to a panel of five international experts. Their answer was unequivocal: the lands transferred in 1898 and 1912 are an unrestricted and integral part of Quebec territory.

The experts based their opinion on legislation passed by the Canadian and Quebec governments to put the James Bay Agreement into effect in 1975. They also pointed out that the aboriginal peoples of these lands renounced their traditional rights under the terms of article 2.1 of the James Bay Agreement: "The James Bay Crees and Inuit of Quebec hereby cede, release, surrender and convey all their Native claims, rights, titles and interests, whatever they may be, in and to land in the Territory and in Quebec, and Quebec and Canada accept such surrender."

The same panel of experts concluded that in the case of a hypothetical claim aimed at dismembering Quebec's territory, the principle of judicial continuity would lead to the conclusion that the territorial integrity of Quebec, guaranteed both by Canadian constitutional law and by international law, should prevail. In short, unless Quebec explicitly authorizes a change in its borders, its territory at the time it becomes sovereign will coincide with the territory it currently holds as a province within the Canadian federation.

Quebec will also need to take measures to guarantee the security of its territory. In this spirit, it will maintain armed forces proportionate to its size and needs. It will also assume its responsibilities in collective security and defence through existing international organizations such as the North Atlantic Treaty Organization (NATO) and the North American Aerospace Defence Command (NORAD).

Continuity of Law

When Quebec becomes sovereign, its state will be entrusted with all the powers and responsibilities that modern states assume. In addition to the powers and responsibilities it now exercises as a province, it will assume the powers now exercised by the federal government in Quebec through Ottawa's exclusive and shared responsibilities and the federal spending power. How will Quebec manage this transition?

To avoid a legal hiatus, the government will propose that the National Assembly maintain federal legislation — such as the Criminal Code or the Bankruptcy Act — in effect until it can amend or recast these laws. In this way, the continuity of judicial proceedings that involve federal jurisdiction and are underway at the time Quebec becomes sovereign can be ensured. Whatever courts have to render judgement in these cases can then do so according to the provisions of the federal legislation in effect at the time they were undertaken.

Continuity of Service to Individuals and Corporations

The Quebec government will prepare appropriate legislative, regulatory and administrative measures to ensure continuity of the services the federal government provides to individuals and corporations. It will take special care to establish mechanisms to avoid any interruption in payment of old age pensions, child tax benefits, unemployment insurance claims, veterans' financial assistance to aboriginal peoples, et cetera. Since Quebec will recover all taxes, it will be able to ensure that these services are maintained. Indeed, it will be able to do so at lower cost through the elimination of duplication and overlap and through the rationalization of some expenses.

It is important here to recall and reiterate the Parti Québécois's firm commitment to provide a job in the Quebec civil service for any federal civil servant from Quebec. The integration of federal civil servants into the Quebec civil service will make available the human resources needed to maintain services and take charge of new responsibilities.

Dividing Public Property and the Debt

Some commentators have long maintained that the question of division of public property and the federal debt when Quebec becomes sovereign involves major difficulties. The Bélanger-Campeau Commission and the National Assembly committee on sovereignty have brought some very pertinent reasoning to bear on this question.

As a matter of principle, a sovereign Quebec would become the owner of federal property within its borders without being required to pay an indemnity. In principle as well, Quebec would not be formally bound by the debt accumulated by the Canadian federal government. However, recognizing that part of the debt was incurred for its benefit, Quebec intends to share it.

In this spirit, the Bélanger-Campeau Commission worked out a methodology for dividing federal property and the debt. This methodology leads to the conclusion that through the combined effect of the recovery of Quebec taxes paid to Ottawa, the transfer of federal services, the division of federal property and the debt, and the elimination of duplication and overlap, Quebec's finances would become significantly healthier.

While limiting its work to only two examples, the Bélanger-Campeau Commission gave some indication of the possible impact of eliminating duplication and overlap. It identified potential annual savings of $522 million relating only to transportation and communication costs and the expenditures of the federal Department of Revenue.

In addition, in the fall of 1990, the Quebec government launched department-by-department studies of the impact of recovering federal services. Despite the relevance of these studies, the government has so far refused to publish their content or conclusions.

International Relations

Quebec will quickly have to become part of the dense and complex fabric of multilateral relations among governments. Its first initiative will be its application for admission to the United Nations. Along with this application, Quebec will also immediately apply for membership in the major UN specialized agencies: the United Nations Educational, Scientific and Cultural Organization (UNESCO), the World

Health Organization (WHO), the International Labor Organization (ILO) and the UN Food and Agriculture Organization (FAO), as well as in some major technical organizations such as the International Civil Aviation Organization (ICAO), whose headquarters are in Montreal. Quebec will also apply for membership in the General Agreement on Tariffs and Trade (GATT), the World Bank, the International Monetary Fund (IMF) and the Organization for Economic Cooperation and Development (OECD).

It goes without saying that Quebec attaches special importance to its participation in the Agence de Coopération Culturelle et Technique — the organization of Francophone countries — and Francophone summits. In these forums, Quebec's status would naturally change from that of "participating government" to that of full member. Quebec will also seek to belong to the Organization of American States, the Commonwealth and the Conference on Security and Cooperation in Europe.

In bilateral relations, ties with Canada will clearly be given top priority. In addition to the close economic relations that they will continue to maintain, Quebec and Canada have numerous interests and concerns in common, in areas as diverse as the environment, territorial defence and security, and transportation and communications. The task will be to define a new relationship on the basis of the historic ties between the two political communities. Thus, attention should be devoted to developing a framework of active cooperation between Quebec and Canada's Francophone minorities and between

Quebec's Anglophone minority and the Anglophone majority in Canada. Cooperation should also be encouraged, to the extent that they wish it, between the aboriginal nations of Quebec and Canada.

Next on the priority list come the United States and France, roughly equal in importance although they have very different relationships with Quebec. Quebec's relations with the United States will be characterized by growing integration in the commercial, financial and industrial spheres. For a number of years now, Quebec's sales to the United States have been growing much more quickly than its sales to the rest of Canada — that is, they have been growing along a north-south rather than an east-west axis.

This process of integration, so characteristic of our era, will continue and broaden. The North American Free Trade Agreement has begun to incorporate Mexico into the North American sphere, and Chile, Colombia and Venezuela have already indicated their desire to become part of NAFTA. It will be very natural for Quebec to take its place in the continental framework. There is nothing theoretical or abstract about this conclusion. Total Quebec-U.S. trade (exports and imports) is equal to half of total Mexico-U.S. trade, nine times total Chile-U.S. trade, and twice total Brazil-U.S. trade. It is close to the level of trade that the United States maintains with France or Italy.

In the economic sphere, Quebec's relations with France will not be as intense as its relations with the United States. However, what France and Quebec can offer each other as ports of entry into their respective continents should not be ignored. In the areas of cultural life, communications, education and research, the community of Francophone countries offers immense possibilities.

Economic Association with Canada

That having been said, we must turn to what is quite properly Quebecers' leading concern with regard to sovereignty: economic association with Canada.

The intensity of economic exchange between Quebec and Canada makes maintaining the Canadian economic space a major consideration when we look at Quebec's accession to sovereignty. A broad consensus in Quebec favours maintaining this space. Preserving it is in Canada's interest as well, irrespective of the political systems prevailing in Canada and Quebec. As a result, the Quebec government will propose concluding an economic association treaty or sectoral agreements that would maintain the Canadian economic space as it currently exists.

This does not exclude the possibility of improving the economic space through subsequent negotiations. However, to ensure a smooth transition, it would be more useful and easier to seek to preserve it as it is than to try to renegotiate all its elements. By maintaining their economic union, Canada and Quebec would be entering into one of the most advanced forms of economic integration between sovereign states anywhere in the world.

The interests of Quebec and Canada in maintaining the economic union dovetail completely. Quebec constitutes the rest of Canada's second largest export market, behind the United States but far ahead of any other country in the world. According to Statistics Canada, Quebec bought merchandise worth more than $20 billion from the rest of Canada in 1988.

The Canadian economic space consists of a number of elements. First, it includes a monetary union, with the Canadian dollar as the common currency. Second, a customs union provides for free movement of goods between Quebec and Canada and a common trade policy towards other countries, making it unnecessary to set up customs posts between the partners. Finally, free movement — in varying degrees — of services, capital and people round out the economic space and make it a form of common market.

Through the work of the Bélanger-Campeau Commission and the National Assembly committee on sovereignty, it has been established that Quebec could maintain a number of the components of the Canadian economic space unilaterally.

The arguments put forward by detractors of Quebec sovereignty have long drawn on the anticipated difficulties of creating a Quebec currency. However, it has been established that Quebec could technically continue to use the Canadian dollar as its currency without anyone being able to stop it. Against that point, it has frequently been argued that if Quebec followed this course, it could not demand participation in setting monetary policy through the Bank of Canada. It is worth pointing out that since the establishment of the Canadian dollar, Quebec has never participated in the conduct of monetary policy. In any event, maintaining a common currency would represent a significant guarantee of stability.

At least some freedom of movement is a characteristic of the Canadian economic space. However, it takes different forms depending on whether it applies to capital, goods, services or people. Everyone recognizes that it would be completely futile if not impossible to try to restrict the free movement of capital. With regard to the free movement of goods and services, it is clearly in the mutual interest of Quebecers and Canadians to maintain the existing customs union and free trade area. Canada might want to limit this aspect of the economic space to a free trade area alone. This would not present insurmountable problems as free movement would still be protected.

Nor does a sovereign Quebec's membership in GATT involve any special problems. Since it was founded in the late 1940s, GATT has brought about a remarkable lowering of the obstacles to international trade. The recently concluded Uruguay Round will further reduce the obstacles that remain. As a member of GATT, Quebec will enjoy significant guaranteed access to international markets, including Canada's.

Membership in GATT will permit Quebec to take advantage of the "most-favoured-nation" clause. Under this clause, a country is required to offer every one of its trading partners treatment equivalent to the best treatment it offers any other country.

Free movement of people is a significant aspect of economic association. It is especially important for inhabitants of border regions who live in one country and work in a neighbouring one on a daily basis. A situation of this sort currently exists between Canada and the United States, and this aspect of the movement of people is managed through international agreements. It would be entirely possible to establish agreements of the same kind between Canada and Quebec.

The question of dual citizenship arises in the same context. Current Canadian legislation recognizes the right to hold more than one citizenship. A sovereign Quebec will follow the same policy. Many Quebecers will apply to the Canadian government to maintain their Canadian citizenship. It is hardly likely that the Canadian government would decide to amend its legislation to allow for dual citizenship with every country except Quebec.

Maintenance of a Canada-Quebec economic space raises the question of how that space should be managed. There are a variety of actions that governments can take in this regard. The governments concerned can simply establish rules by which they are expected to abide. Another course is to establish formal dispute settlement mechanisms. Or governments can pool a portion of their powers by setting up institutions responsible for exercising those powers.

As an example of how this would work, the establishment of three major joint institutions could be envisaged. First, a council composed of ministers or representatives designated and delegated by the two countries could exercise decision-making power in matters specified under the economic association treaty. Second, a secretariat could be responsible for applying the treaty according to the directives of the council. Finally, a tribunal could be in charge of settling disputes. A form of Quebec participation in the Bank of Canada could also be provided for. The ministers or delegates who would sit on the council would remain responsible to their respective parliaments, ensuring democratic control of the treaty or treaties governing the activity of these bodies.

Joint commissions responsible for managing specialized aspects of the association treaty could also be envisaged. For instance, a commission could oversee the rules concerning the transfer of pensions or specific environmental or transportation issues involving the two countries. All these questions should be approached with an open mind and with the goal of ensuring that a treaty providing for maintenance of the Canadian economic space is applied in the best possible way.

It is in the interest of both Quebec and Canada to make sure that the transition takes place as smoothly as possible and that the mechanisms set up to manage their mutual relations are as effective as they can be. They both have everything to gain in remaining receptive to proposals from the other partner so that they can quickly reach mutually advantageous common ground.

Conclusion

Never in history has Quebec seemed so close to attaining political sovereignty. An ideal that the Parti Québécois has been working to define and promote for twenty-five years is now within reach.

Changes in the organization of the world offer new opportunities for any society that can mobilize its resources. The great lesson of the second half of the twentieth century is that, with the development of large international economic units, small peoples can now achieve progress and make a contribution that is fully commensurate with their capabilities so long as they are integrated into these large markets.

The referendum of October 26, 1992 confirmed once again that it is impossible to renew the Canadian federal system in a way that takes the interests of both Quebec and English Canada into account. Quebecers said No to a proposal that they regarded as inadequate and in some respects even dangerous. For English Canadians, too much was being conceded to Quebec while changes directed more specifically to their needs did not go far enough. After the unilateral repatriation of the constitution in 1982, the rejection of the Meech Lake Accord in 1990 and, finally, the 1992 referendum, the road of renewed federalism has again been shown for what it always was: a dead end.

The inertia of the postreferendum period has left Quebec in a position of weakness. On one level, of course, this is true because inaction perpetuates the status quo that now as always is unacceptable to us. The Bélanger-Campeau Commission rightly evoked "the extent and depth of the consensus that was expressed to the effect that the population of Québec unequivocally rejects the current state of affairs." Even Quebec Premier Robert Bourassa wrote in his addendum to the Bélanger-Campeau Report, "This report confirms for us that in the discussions and decisions regarding the political and constitutional future of Québec two avenues of action must be considered simultaneously: an in-depth reorganization of the existing federal system, or sovereignty for Québec." The report of the constitutional committee of the Liberal Party of Quebec — the Allaire Report — went even further. The Allaire Report established two objectives: to affirm the distinct character of Quebec society and to strengthen Quebec economically. Then it stated, "The constitutional status quo seems to threaten both objectives."

The current inertia also puts Quebec in a position of weakness because it is synonymous with abdication and surrender. Before the Quebec government resigned itself to accepting the Charlottetown Accord, all of Quebec had defined what it considered essential for its development. Even people who wanted to give federalism another last chance demanded changes that were completely incommensurate with what the Quebec government finally accepted. The Bélanger-Campeau Report recommended that a referendum be held on the sovereignty of Quebec. The Quebec National Assembly passed Bill 150, of which a referendum on sovereignty was the central point. Even the Quebec Liberal Party fell into line at its March 1991 convention.

For the Quebec government, remaining silent after the rejection of Charlottetown means renouncing everything: our aspirations and our desire for progress. It means renouncing the possibility of a thriving Quebec while accepting federalism as it is, even after explicitly acknowledging that this solution can never be acceptable for our society. The submissiveness of the Quebec government cannot and must not become the submissiveness of Quebec.

That is why it is urgent to achieve Quebec sovereignty as rapidly as possible. However, there is no chance that political leaders currently in office will propose this course to Quebecers. On the other hand, whatever attitude current governments may take, there are opportunities for citizens to restate this long-awaited goal and make it concrete.

The first of these came in the federal election of October 25, 1993. In previous federal elections, Quebecers' choices had almost always been limited to choosing among federalist parties or spoiling their ballots. This time, in voting for the Bloc Québécois, they had a genuine and virtually unprecedented opportunity to use their votes to move towards a sovereign Quebec.

A second vote will take place in 1994: the Quebec election. There will be a very clear choice. On the one hand, there is the Liberal Party, which after a series of hesitations and rifts has repudiated the Allaire Report and fallen back on a very orthodox conception of Canadian federalism. On the other hand, there is the Parti Québécois, which is sovereignist "before, during and after elections." If this election results in the Parti Québécois being called on to form a government, a referendum will be held in 1995 to achieve sovereignty.

These successive encounters provide Quebecers with a singular opportunity to take a decisive turn in their history. The generations that constitute Quebec today are invited to do more than make a choice between political options. They are called to define the inheritance that they intend to leave to their children and the generations to come.

Quebec society is being buffeted from all sides. It is caught up in a worldwide current and is criss-crossed by new trends that are redefining its economy, culture and networks of solidarity. And this is only a beginning. The pace of change is destined to increase, not to diminish. We must not only adjust to changes that have already taken place, but must also face those yet to come. The political choices we make now should be directed towards increasing the capacity of Quebec's young people and the generations to come to be masters of their own destiny and pursue their own aspirations. History will judge whether we fulfilled our responsibility to provide them with this capacity to act.

Quebec society cannot avoid these challenges. To respond to them, it must mobilize fully and have at its disposal the instruments it needs to define its development strategies. These challenges can open up untold possibilities for us. But without the tools that only sovereignty can provide, they will appear to us, in the end, as threats that sap our capacity for action.

Never in its history has Quebec faced such exciting possibilities. This new world is our world too. We can and must contribute towards building it. If we have the means to fulfil our ambitions, we will make an original contribution to what is increasingly becoming the *projet de société* of all humanity.

Canada shares this challenge with us. Canada too must find its place in the new world environment and have the leeway it needs to carry out its choices. No less than Quebec, Canada pays the price of belonging to an obsolete and crippling political system. Canada too faces an urgent need to change things so that it can recover the capacity to act in its own way and at its own pace.

In this context, the proposal to make Quebec a sovereign state is aimed primarily at giving us the capacity to adapt and the instruments of our emancipation. It has nothing to do with drawing new political borders in a world where such borders are slowly losing the significance that history once gave them. On the contrary, it means getting rid of the borders that are blocking our progress and our partners' progress as well. In doing this, we will recover our capacity to act, gather together our power to be ourselves, and find in ourselves the extra spirit that we need to build a new society in a new world.

We must keep our appointment with destiny.

Members of the National Executive Council of the Parti Québécois

At the Time the French Edition Was Written

Jacques Parizeau
President of the Parti Québécois
Bernard Landry
President of the National Executive Council and first vice-president of the Parti Québécois
Paul Bégin
Second vice-president and president of the National Office
Francine Lalonde
Councillor responsible for the party platform
Rita Dionne-Marsolais
Treasurer
Jeanne Blackburn
Councillor and member of the National Assembly
Guy Chevrette
Councillor and member of the National Assembly
Roger Paré
Councillor and member of the National Assembly
David Cliche
Councillor
Jocelyne Gadbois
Councillor
Camille Laurin
Councillor

As of February 1994

Jacques Parizeau
President of the Parti Québécois
Bernard Landry
President of the National Executive Council and first vice-president of the Parti Québécois
Paul Bégin
Second vice-president and president of the National Office
Giuseppe Sciortino
Councillor responsible for the party platform
Rita Dionne-Marsolais
Treasurer
Jeanne Blackburn
Councillor and member of the National Assembly
André Boisclair
Councillor and member of the National Assembly
Guy Chevrette
Councillor and member of the National Assembly
Jean Campeau
Councillor
Jocelyne Gadbois
Councillor
Carmen Sabag-Vaillancourt
Councillor
Christian Picard
President of the National Youth Committee

Printed by
Ateliers Graphiques Marc Veilleux Inc.
Cap-Saint-Ignace, Québec
in March 1994.

DATE DUE